Password

LOGBOOK

O'BRIEN
PUBLISHING
COPYRIGHT 2021

D1410197

Password
TIPS

 Make your password long.

 Avoid using personal information.

 Include numbers, upper case, lower case, and special symbols.

 Use a different password for each site.

 Do not share your password with others.

 Change your password regularly.

Passwords

Website

Username	
Password	
Email	
Notes	

Website

Username	
Password	
Email	
Notes	

Website

Username	
Password	
Email	
Notes	

Website

Username	
Password	
Email	
Notes	

A Passwords

Website

Username	
Password	
Email	
Notes	

Website

Username	
Password	
Email	
Notes	

Website

Username	
Password	
Email	
Notes	

Website

Username	
Password	
Email	
Notes	

Passwords

Website
Username	
Password	
Email	
Notes	

Website
Username	
Password	
Email	
Notes	

Website
Username	
Password	
Email	
Notes	

Website
Username	
Password	
Email	
Notes	

A Passwords

Website

Username	
Password	
Email	
Notes	

Website

Username	
Password	
Email	
Notes	

Website

Username	
Password	
Email	
Notes	

Website

Username	
Password	
Email	
Notes	

Passwords

Website

Username	
Password	
Email	
Notes	

Website

Username	
Password	
Email	
Notes	

Website

Username	
Password	
Email	
Notes	

Website

Username	
Password	
Email	
Notes	

B

Passwords

Website

Username	
Password	
Email	
Notes	

Website

Username	
Password	
Email	
Notes	

Website

Username	
Password	
Email	
Notes	

Website

Username	
Password	
Email	
Notes	

Passwords

Website

Username	
Password	
Email	
Notes	

Website

Username	
Password	
Email	
Notes	

Website

Username	
Password	
Email	
Notes	

Website

Username	
Password	
Email	
Notes	

B

Passwords

Website

Username	
Password	
Email	
Notes	

Website

Username	
Password	
Email	
Notes	

Website

Username	
Password	
Email	
Notes	

Website

Username	
Password	
Email	
Notes	

Passwords

Website

Username	
Password	
Email	
Notes	

Website

Username	
Password	
Email	
Notes	

Website

Username	
Password	
Email	
Notes	

Website

Username	
Password	
Email	
Notes	

C Passwords

Website

Username	
Password	
Email	
Notes	

Website

Username	
Password	
Email	
Notes	

Website

Username	
Password	
Email	
Notes	

Website

Username	
Password	
Email	
Notes	

Passwords

Website

Username	
Password	
Email	
Notes	

Website

Username	
Password	
Email	
Notes	

Website

Username	
Password	
Email	
Notes	

Website

Username	
Password	
Email	
Notes	

C   Passwords

Website

Username	
Password	
Email	
Notes	

Website

Username	
Password	
Email	
Notes	

Website

Username	
Password	
Email	
Notes	

Website

Username	
Password	
Email	
Notes	

Passwords

Website

Username	
Password	
Email	
Notes	

Website

Username	
Password	
Email	
Notes	

Website

Username	
Password	
Email	
Notes	

Website

Username	
Password	
Email	
Notes	

Passwords

Website

Username	
Password	
Email	
Notes	

Website

Username	
Password	
Email	
Notes	

Website

Username	
Password	
Email	
Notes	

Website

Username	
Password	
Email	
Notes	

Passwords

Website
Username	
Password	
Email	
Notes	

Website
Username	
Password	
Email	
Notes	

Website
Username	
Password	
Email	
Notes	

Website
Username	
Password	
Email	
Notes	

D Passwords

Website

Username	
Password	
Email	
Notes	

Website

Username	
Password	
Email	
Notes	

Website

Username	
Password	
Email	
Notes	

Website

Username	
Password	
Email	
Notes	

Passwords

Website

Username	
Password	
Email	
Notes	

Website

Username	
Password	
Email	
Notes	

Website

Username	
Password	
Email	
Notes	

Website

Username	
Password	
Email	
Notes	

E

Passwords

Website

Username	
Password	
Email	
Notes	

Website

Username	
Password	
Email	
Notes	

Website

Username	
Password	
Email	
Notes	

Website

Username	
Password	
Email	
Notes	

Passwords

E

Website

Username	
Password	
Email	
Notes	

Website

Username	
Password	
Email	
Notes	

Website

Username	
Password	
Email	
Notes	

Website

Username	
Password	
Email	
Notes	

E

Passwords

Website

Username	
Password	
Email	
Notes	

Website

Username	
Password	
Email	
Notes	

Website

Username	
Password	
Email	
Notes	

Website

Username	
Password	
Email	
Notes	

Passwords

Website

Username	
Password	
Email	
Notes	

Website

Username	
Password	
Email	
Notes	

Website

Username	
Password	
Email	
Notes	

Website

Username	
Password	
Email	
Notes	

Passwords

Website

Username	
Password	
Email	
Notes	

Website

Username	
Password	
Email	
Notes	

Website

Username	
Password	
Email	
Notes	

Website

Username	
Password	
Email	
Notes	

Passwords

Website

Username	
Password	
Email	
Notes	

Website

Username	
Password	
Email	
Notes	

Website

Username	
Password	
Email	
Notes	

Website

Username	
Password	
Email	
Notes	

Passwords

Website

Username	
Password	
Email	
Notes	

Website

Username	
Password	
Email	
Notes	

Website

Username	
Password	
Email	
Notes	

Website

Username	
Password	
Email	
Notes	

Passwords G

Website
Username	
Password	
Email	
Notes	

Website
Username	
Password	
Email	
Notes	

Website
Username	
Password	
Email	
Notes	

Website
Username	
Password	
Email	
Notes	

G   Passwords

Website
Username	
Password	
Email	
Notes	

Website
Username	
Password	
Email	
Notes	

Website
Username	
Password	
Email	
Notes	

Website
Username	
Password	
Email	
Notes	

Passwords

G

Website

Username	
Password	
Email	
Notes	

Website

Username	
Password	
Email	
Notes	

Website

Username	
Password	
Email	
Notes	

Website

Username	
Password	
Email	
Notes	

G Passwords

Website

Username	
Password	
Email	
Notes	

Website

Username	
Password	
Email	
Notes	

Website

Username	
Password	
Email	
Notes	

Website

Username	
Password	
Email	
Notes	

Passwords

Website

Username	
Password	
Email	
Notes	

Website

Username	
Password	
Email	
Notes	

Website

Username	
Password	
Email	
Notes	

Website

Username	
Password	
Email	
Notes	

H

Passwords

Website

Username	
Password	
Email	
Notes	

Website

Username	
Password	
Email	
Notes	

Website

Username	
Password	
Email	
Notes	

Website

Username	
Password	
Email	
Notes	

Passwords

Website

Username	
Password	
Email	
Notes	

Website

Username	
Password	
Email	
Notes	

Website

Username	
Password	
Email	
Notes	

Website

Username	
Password	
Email	
Notes	

H   Passwords

Website

Username	
Password	
Email	
Notes	

Website

Username	
Password	
Email	
Notes	

Website

Username	
Password	
Email	
Notes	

Website

Username	
Password	
Email	
Notes	

Passwords

Website

Username	
Password	
Email	
Notes	

Website

Username	
Password	
Email	
Notes	

Website

Username	
Password	
Email	
Notes	

Website

Username	
Password	
Email	
Notes	

Passwords

Website

Username	
Password	
Email	
Notes	

Website

Username	
Password	
Email	
Notes	

Website

Username	
Password	
Email	
Notes	

Website

Username	
Password	
Email	
Notes	

Passwords

Website

Username	
Password	
Email	
Notes	

Website

Username	
Password	
Email	
Notes	

Website

Username	
Password	
Email	
Notes	

Website

Username	
Password	
Email	
Notes	

Passwords

Website
Username	
Password	
Email	
Notes	

Website
Username	
Password	
Email	
Notes	

Website
Username	
Password	
Email	
Notes	

Website
Username	
Password	
Email	
Notes	

Passwords $\mathcal{J}$

Website
Username	
Password	
Email	
Notes	

Website
Username	
Password	
Email	
Notes	

Website
Username	
Password	
Email	
Notes	

Website
Username	
Password	
Email	
Notes	

J   Passwords

Website

Username	
Password	
Email	
Notes	

Website

Username	
Password	
Email	
Notes	

Website

Username	
Password	
Email	
Notes	

Website

Username	
Password	
Email	
Notes	

Passwords
J

Website
Username	
Password	
Email	
Notes	

Website
Username	
Password	
Email	
Notes	

Website
Username	
Password	
Email	
Notes	

Website
Username	
Password	
Email	
Notes	

J Passwords

Website

Username	
Password	
Email	
Notes	

Website

Username	
Password	
Email	
Notes	

Website

Username	
Password	
Email	
Notes	

Website

Username	
Password	
Email	
Notes	

Passwords

Website
Username	
Password	
Email	
Notes	

Website
Username	
Password	
Email	
Notes	

Website
Username	
Password	
Email	
Notes	

Website
Username	
Password	
Email	
Notes	

K   Passwords

Website

Username	
Password	
Email	
Notes	

Website

Username	
Password	
Email	
Notes	

Website

Username	
Password	
Email	
Notes	

Website

Username	
Password	
Email	
Notes	

Passwords

K

Website

Username	
Password	
Email	
Notes	

Website

Username	
Password	
Email	
Notes	

Website

Username	
Password	
Email	
Notes	

Website

Username	
Password	
Email	
Notes	

K

Passwords

Website

Username	
Password	
Email	
Notes	

Website

Username	
Password	
Email	
Notes	

Website

Username	
Password	
Email	
Notes	

Website

Username	
Password	
Email	
Notes	

Passwords

L

Website

Username	
Password	
Email	
Notes	

Website

Username	
Password	
Email	
Notes	

Website

Username	
Password	
Email	
Notes	

Website

Username	
Password	
Email	
Notes	

L   Passwords

Website
Username	
Password	
Email	
Notes	

Website
Username	
Password	
Email	
Notes	

Website
Username	
Password	
Email	
Notes	

Website
Username	
Password	
Email	
Notes	

Passwords

L

Website

Username	
Password	
Email	
Notes	

Website

Username	
Password	
Email	
Notes	

Website

Username	
Password	
Email	
Notes	

Website

Username	
Password	
Email	
Notes	

L Passwords

Website

Username	
Password	
Email	
Notes	

Website

Username	
Password	
Email	
Notes	

Website

Username	
Password	
Email	
Notes	

Website

Username	
Password	
Email	
Notes	

Passwords

Website

Username	
Password	
Email	
Notes	

Website

Username	
Password	
Email	
Notes	

Website

Username	
Password	
Email	
Notes	

Website

Username	
Password	
Email	
Notes	

M

Passwords

Website

Username	
Password	
Email	
Notes	

Website

Username	
Password	
Email	
Notes	

Website

Username	
Password	
Email	
Notes	

Website

Username	
Password	
Email	
Notes	

Passwords

M

Website

Username	
Password	
Email	
Notes	

Website

Username	
Password	
Email	
Notes	

Website

Username	
Password	
Email	
Notes	

Website

Username	
Password	
Email	
Notes	

M

Passwords

Website

Username	
Password	
Email	
Notes	

Website

Username	
Password	
Email	
Notes	

Website

Username	
Password	
Email	
Notes	

Website

Username	
Password	
Email	
Notes	

Passwords

Website

Username	
Password	
Email	
Notes	

Website

Username	
Password	
Email	
Notes	

Website

Username	
Password	
Email	
Notes	

Website

Username	
Password	
Email	
Notes	

N

Passwords

Website

Username	
Password	
Email	
Notes	

Website

Username	
Password	
Email	
Notes	

Website

Username	
Password	
Email	
Notes	

Website

Username	
Password	
Email	
Notes	

Passwords

Website

Username	
Password	
Email	
Notes	

Website

Username	
Password	
Email	
Notes	

Website

Username	
Password	
Email	
Notes	

Website

Username	
Password	
Email	
Notes	

N

Passwords

Website

Username	
Password	
Email	
Notes	

Website

Username	
Password	
Email	
Notes	

Website

Username	
Password	
Email	
Notes	

Website

Username	
Password	
Email	
Notes	

Passwords

Website

Username	
Password	
Email	
Notes	

Website

Username	
Password	
Email	
Notes	

Website

Username	
Password	
Email	
Notes	

Website

Username	
Password	
Email	
Notes	

O   Passwords

Website

Username	
Password	
Email	
Notes	

Website

Username	
Password	
Email	
Notes	

Website

Username	
Password	
Email	
Notes	

Website

Username	
Password	
Email	
Notes	

Passwords

Website

Username	
Password	
Email	
Notes	

Website

Username	
Password	
Email	
Notes	

Website

Username	
Password	
Email	
Notes	

Website

Username	
Password	
Email	
Notes	

O Passwords

Website

Username	
Password	
Email	
Notes	

Website

Username	
Password	
Email	
Notes	

Website

Username	
Password	
Email	
Notes	

Website

Username	
Password	
Email	
Notes	

Passwords

P

Website

Username	
Password	
Email	
Notes	

Website

Username	
Password	
Email	
Notes	

Website

Username	
Password	
Email	
Notes	

Website

Username	
Password	
Email	
Notes	

P   Passwords

Website
Username	
Password	
Email	
Notes	

Website
Username	
Password	
Email	
Notes	

Website
Username	
Password	
Email	
Notes	

Website
Username	
Password	
Email	
Notes	

Passwords

Website

Username	
Password	
Email	
Notes	

Website

Username	
Password	
Email	
Notes	

Website

Username	
Password	
Email	
Notes	

Website

Username	
Password	
Email	
Notes	

P   Passwords

Website

Username	
Password	
Email	
Notes	

Website

Username	
Password	
Email	
Notes	

Website

Username	
Password	
Email	
Notes	

Website

Username	
Password	
Email	
Notes	

Passwords

Website
Username	
Password	
Email	
Notes	

Website
Username	
Password	
Email	
Notes	

Website
Username	
Password	
Email	
Notes	

Website
Username	
Password	
Email	
Notes	

Q   Passwords

Website

Username	
Password	
Email	
Notes	

Website

Username	
Password	
Email	
Notes	

Website

Username	
Password	
Email	
Notes	

Website

Username	
Password	
Email	
Notes	

Passwords

Q

Website

Username	
Password	
Email	
Notes	

Website

Username	
Password	
Email	
Notes	

Website

Username	
Password	
Email	
Notes	

Website

Username	
Password	
Email	
Notes	

Q   Passwords

Website

Username	
Password	
Email	
Notes	

Website

Username	
Password	
Email	
Notes	

Website

Username	
Password	
Email	
Notes	

Website

Username	
Password	
Email	
Notes	

Passwords

Website

Username	
Password	
Email	
Notes	

Website

Username	
Password	
Email	
Notes	

Website

Username	
Password	
Email	
Notes	

Website

Username	
Password	
Email	
Notes	

R

Passwords

Website

Username	
Password	
Email	
Notes	

Website

Username	
Password	
Email	
Notes	

Website

Username	
Password	
Email	
Notes	

Website

Username	
Password	
Email	
Notes	

Passwords

R

Website

Username	
Password	
Email	
Notes	

Website

Username	
Password	
Email	
Notes	

Website

Username	
Password	
Email	
Notes	

Website

Username	
Password	
Email	
Notes	

R

Passwords

Website

Username	
Password	
Email	
Notes	

Website

Username	
Password	
Email	
Notes	

Website

Username	
Password	
Email	
Notes	

Website

Username	
Password	
Email	
Notes	

Passwords

Website

Username	
Password	
Email	
Notes	

Website

Username	
Password	
Email	
Notes	

Website

Username	
Password	
Email	
Notes	

Website

Username	
Password	
Email	
Notes	

S   Passwords

Website

Username	
Password	
Email	
Notes	

Website

Username	
Password	
Email	
Notes	

Website

Username	
Password	
Email	
Notes	

Website

Username	
Password	
Email	
Notes	

Passwords

Website

Username	
Password	
Email	
Notes	

Website

Username	
Password	
Email	
Notes	

Website

Username	
Password	
Email	
Notes	

Website

Username	
Password	
Email	
Notes	

S   Passwords

Website
Username	
Password	
Email	
Notes	

Website
Username	
Password	
Email	
Notes	

Website
Username	
Password	
Email	
Notes	

Website
Username	
Password	
Email	
Notes	

Passwords

T

Website
Username	
Password	
Email	
Notes	

Website
Username	
Password	
Email	
Notes	

Website
Username	
Password	
Email	
Notes	

Website
Username	
Password	
Email	
Notes	

T   Passwords

Website

Username	
Password	
Email	
Notes	

Website

Username	
Password	
Email	
Notes	

Website

Username	
Password	
Email	
Notes	

Website

Username	
Password	
Email	
Notes	

Passwords

T

Website
Username	
Password	
Email	
Notes	

Website
Username	
Password	
Email	
Notes	

Website
Username	
Password	
Email	
Notes	

Website
Username	
Password	
Email	
Notes	

T   Passwords

Website

Username	
Password	
Email	
Notes	

Website

Username	
Password	
Email	
Notes	

Website

Username	
Password	
Email	
Notes	

Website

Username	
Password	
Email	
Notes	

Passwords U

Website
Username	
Password	
Email	
Notes	

Website
Username	
Password	
Email	
Notes	

Website
Username	
Password	
Email	
Notes	

Website
Username	
Password	
Email	
Notes	

U   Passwords

Website

Username	
Password	
Email	
Notes	

Website

Username	
Password	
Email	
Notes	

Website

Username	
Password	
Email	
Notes	

Website

Username	
Password	
Email	
Notes	

Passwords

U

Website

Username	
Password	
Email	
Notes	

Website

Username	
Password	
Email	
Notes	

Website

Username	
Password	
Email	
Notes	

Website

Username	
Password	
Email	
Notes	

U   Passwords

Website

Username	
Password	
Email	
Notes	

Website

Username	
Password	
Email	
Notes	

Website

Username	
Password	
Email	
Notes	

Website

Username	
Password	
Email	
Notes	

Passwords

V

Website
Username	
Password	
Email	
Notes	

Website
Username	
Password	
Email	
Notes	

Website
Username	
Password	
Email	
Notes	

Website
Username	
Password	
Email	
Notes	

V   Passwords

Website

Username	
Password	
Email	
Notes	

Website

Username	
Password	
Email	
Notes	

Website

Username	
Password	
Email	
Notes	

Website

Username	
Password	
Email	
Notes	

Passwords

V

Website

Username	
Password	
Email	
Notes	

Website

Username	
Password	
Email	
Notes	

Website

Username	
Password	
Email	
Notes	

Website

Username	
Password	
Email	
Notes	

V Passwords

Website

Username	
Password	
Email	
Notes	

Website

Username	
Password	
Email	
Notes	

Website

Username	
Password	
Email	
Notes	

Website

Username	
Password	
Email	
Notes	

Passwords

W

Website

Username	
Password	
Email	
Notes	

Website

Username	
Password	
Email	
Notes	

Website

Username	
Password	
Email	
Notes	

Website

Username	
Password	
Email	
Notes	

W   Passwords

Website

Username	
Password	
Email	
Notes	

Website

Username	
Password	
Email	
Notes	

Website

Username	
Password	
Email	
Notes	

Website

Username	
Password	
Email	
Notes	

Passwords

W

Website

Username	
Password	
Email	
Notes	

Website

Username	
Password	
Email	
Notes	

Website

Username	
Password	
Email	
Notes	

Website

Username	
Password	
Email	
Notes	

W   Passwords

Website

Username	
Password	
Email	
Notes	

Website

Username	
Password	
Email	
Notes	

Website

Username	
Password	
Email	
Notes	

Website

Username	
Password	
Email	
Notes	

Passwords

X

Website

Username	
Password	
Email	
Notes	

Website

Username	
Password	
Email	
Notes	

Website

Username	
Password	
Email	
Notes	

Website

Username	
Password	
Email	
Notes	

X Passwords

Website

Username	
Password	
Email	
Notes	

Website

Username	
Password	
Email	
Notes	

Website

Username	
Password	
Email	
Notes	

Website

Username	
Password	
Email	
Notes	

Passwords X

Website

Username	
Password	
Email	
Notes	

Website

Username	
Password	
Email	
Notes	

Website

Username	
Password	
Email	
Notes	

Website

Username	
Password	
Email	
Notes	

X   Passwords

Website

Username	
Password	
Email	
Notes	

Website

Username	
Password	
Email	
Notes	

Website

Username	
Password	
Email	
Notes	

Website

Username	
Password	
Email	
Notes	

Passwords

Website

Username	
Password	
Email	
Notes	

Website

Username	
Password	
Email	
Notes	

Website

Username	
Password	
Email	
Notes	

Website

Username	
Password	
Email	
Notes	

Y
Passwords

Website

Username	
Password	
Email	
Notes	

Website

Username	
Password	
Email	
Notes	

Website

Username	
Password	
Email	
Notes	

Website

Username	
Password	
Email	
Notes	

Passwords

Website

Username	
Password	
Email	
Notes	

Website

Username	
Password	
Email	
Notes	

Website

Username	
Password	
Email	
Notes	

Website

Username	
Password	
Email	
Notes	

Y

Passwords

Website

Username	
Password	
Email	
Notes	

Website

Username	
Password	
Email	
Notes	

Website

Username	
Password	
Email	
Notes	

Website

Username	
Password	
Email	
Notes	

Passncords

Z

Website

Username	
Password	
Email	
Notes	

Website

Username	
Password	
Email	
Notes	

Website

Username	
Password	
Email	
Notes	

Website

Username	
Password	
Email	
Notes	

Z

Passwords

Website

Username	
Password	
Email	
Notes	

Website

Username	
Password	
Email	
Notes	

Website

Username	
Password	
Email	
Notes	

Website

Username	
Password	
Email	
Notes	

Passwords

Z

Website

Username	
Password	
Email	
Notes	

Website

Username	
Password	
Email	
Notes	

Website

Username	
Password	
Email	
Notes	

Website

Username	
Password	
Email	
Notes	

Z Passwords

Website

Username	
Password	
Email	
Notes	

Website

Username	
Password	
Email	
Notes	

Website

Username	
Password	
Email	
Notes	

Website

Username	
Password	
Email	
Notes	